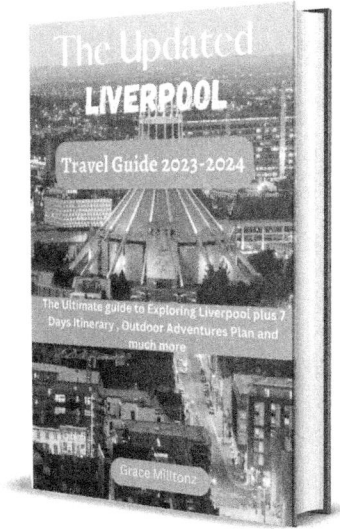

The Updated
LIVERPOOL
Travel Guide 2023-2024

The Ultimate guide to Exploring Liverpool plus 7
Days Itinerary , Outdoor Adventures Plan and
much more

Grace Miltonz

The Updated Liverpool Travel Guide 2023-2024

The Ultimate guide to Exploring Liverpool plus 7 Days Itinerary , Outdoor Adventures Plan and much more

Copyright

Grace Milltonz

Table of Contents

Chapter 1 : Introduction to Liverpool

Liverpool, oh Liverpool! The birthplace of The Beatles and our chosen location for a memorable tourist adventure. Our voyage began with enthusiastic expectation, armed with inquiry, empathy, and a dash of comedy.

We were immediately delighted by the warm Scouse accents that greeted us at every corner when we arrived in this vibrant metropolis. The residents were not only friendly; they were actually enthusiastic about their cherished hometown. It was as if we had discovered a buried treasure trove of stories just waiting to be told.

The recognizable rhythm of the Beatles' oldies floated towards us like a seductive siren's lure as we meandered through the crowded streets. We couldn't resist going straight into the heart of Beatlemania at the Cavern Club. The atmosphere inside was electric, and the supporters' solidarity was contagious. Even non-die-hard fans found themselves humming along to the melodies, recognizing that you can't escape the magnetic draw of the Fab Four in Liverpool.

Our sense of humor came into play as we performed our best John, Paul, George, and Ringo impersonations - believe me, it's more difficult than it appears! We shared an unconscious understanding to leave the singing careers to the experts and laughed heartily at our own cost. We connected with our fellow travelers through our unrestrained laughter, all of us united by our passion for these musical legends.

We looked into Liverpool's maritime heritage in addition to the renowned Beatles sites. With its towering grandeur and busy waterfront ambience, the Royal Albert Dock was a stunning sight. We went to the Merseyside Maritime Museum, where we learned about the city's rich maritime history and empathized with the challenges and successes of sailors over the ages. It was a moving reminder of the human spirit's tenacity.

But our search for the soul of Liverpool didn't stop there. The city's football culture was legendary, and we couldn't resist joining a bunch of fervent supporters for a game at Anfield. As inexperienced soccer fans, we struggled with the chants, shouting at the incorrect times and garnering the amusement of seasoned fans. Nonetheless, the atmosphere and excitement in the stadium made us feel like true Reds, cheering on Liverpool with zeal.

We couldn't help but feel a sense of enchantment in the air as the sun fell over the city's skyline. The history, music, and people we met had weaved a tapestry of experiences that had left an indelible mark on our hearts.

Our fantastic adventure in Liverpool was about more than just visiting tourist sights; it was about embracing the essence of this incredible city. We found ourselves interacting with strangers through common interests and laughing at our own eccentricities. Liverpool's allure stems not only from its storied past, but also from the warmth and wit of its people, making it a destination unlike any other.

So, if you ever find yourself in Liverpool, remember to bring empathy, intrigue, and a healthy dose of humor with you. Embrace the oddities, dance to the music, and immerse yourself in the legends of this city. Liverpool will warmly greet you, and who knows, you might just depart with a song in your heart and a smile on your face!

Chapter 2 : History and Culture of Liverpool

Liverpool, a city rich in history and ornamented with a lively cultural tapestry, stands proudly on the banks of the River Mersey in northwest England. This city is famous for being the birthplace of The Beatles and the iconic Liverpool Football Club, but it is much more than that. Its intriguing past and dynamic present combine to make an astonishing narrative that continues to capture the hearts and minds of those who walk its historic streets.

Liverpool's history can be traced back over 800 years to its humble origins as a fishing community. The city's strategic location near the sea boosted trade and nautical activity, making it into one of the most important ports in the British Empire during the 18th and 19th centuries. The wealth brought in by global trade not only created its economic success, but also drove the city's unique multiculturalism, as waves of immigrants from Ireland, Africa, China, and other corners of the world added to its eclectic identity.

However, Liverpool's wealth was not simply the result of lawful trade. The tragic legacy of the transatlantic slave trade has likewise left an everlasting effect on its history. The city's deep role in the shipping of slaves and commodities throughout the 18th century caused intense disputes and has been a source of remorse and reconciliation in recent times. Today, museums and memorials serve as evocative reminders of this tragic past, encouraging conversation and understanding about the horrors of slavery.

The Beatles Phenomenon: The 1960s saw a cultural explosion in Liverpool, with the advent of the world-famous rock band, The Beatles. John Lennon, Paul McCartney, George Harrison, and Ringo Starr changed the music industry and became global legends. The Cavern Club, where the Beatles began their journey, is still a destination for music fans all around the world. The city is proud of its musical past, with various venues holding live performances and an annual International Beatle Week festival bringing fans and performers from all over the world.

Proud Sporting Traditions: Apart from its musical legacy, Liverpool's cultural identity is also closely entwined with sports, particularly football. The city's football clubs, Liverpool FC and Everton FC, have a fierce rivalry and are among the most successful in the country. The passion of match days, with fans singing in unison and surrounding the city in a sea of red and blue, is a sight to behold.

Beyond music and sports, Liverpool has a flourishing cultural sector, with various galleries, theaters, and performance places. The Tate

Liverpool and the Walker Art Gallery house an extraordinary collection of artworks, while the Everyman and Playhouse Theatres present cutting-edge productions. Literary, dance, and film festivals contribute to the city's cultural attractiveness.

Today, Liverpool is evolving, conserving its legacy while adopting a modern spirit. As you walk through the streets, the various architecture, from prominent buildings like the Royal Liver Building to the majestic St. George's Hall, serves as a visual testament to the city's rich past.

Chapter 3 : Visa Requirements for Liverpool

If you plan to visit Liverpool as a tourist, the visa requirements will vary depending on your nationality and the length of your stay. The United Kingdom has a points-based immigration system that comprises multiple visa categories for different reasons of travel.

European Union (EU) and European Economic Area (EEA) citizens: As per my most recent update in September 2021, EU and EEA citizens might travel to Liverpool and the UK with a valid passport or national ID card. However, due to the UK's exit from the EU (Brexit), there may have been some modifications in the travel laws for EU/EEA people since then. It is critical to obtain the most recent information from official UK government sources.

Visa Waiver Countries: Citizens of various countries outside the EU/EEA may be eligible for visa-free entrance to the UK for short-term tourism purposes. These nations are included on the UK government's official website. Citizens of the United States, Canada, Australia, New Zealand, Japan, and many other countries, for example, may be eligible for visa-free entry for up to six months. They must, however, get an Electronic Travel Authorization (ETA) before traveling.

Non-Visa Waiver Countries: If you are a citizen of a country that is not covered by the visa waiver program, you will need to apply for a Standard Visitor Visa to visit Liverpool for tourism purposes. This visa permits you to stay in the UK for up to six months for leisure, sightseeing, or visiting family and friends.

How to Apply for a UK Standard Visitor Visa:

To apply for a Standard Visitor Visa, you will normally need to complete the following steps:

a. Determine your eligibility: Go to the official UK government website to see if you are qualified for a Standard Visitor Visa.

a. Gather documents: Gather the necessary documents, which may include a valid passport, recent passport-sized pictures, proof of sufficient funds to support yourself during your stay, travel itinerary, hotel details, and any other documents required by the UK embassy or consulate.

c. Apply online: Fill out the online visa application form on the UK government's official website, pay the application fee, and arrange an appointment at your local UK embassy or consulate.

c. Attend the interview: Attend the visa interview, where you may be asked questions regarding your travel plans and goals during your stay in the UK.

b. Wait for a decision: Because the processing period for visa applications varies, it's critical to apply well in advance of your chosen travel date.

Important Reminders:

Always check the official UK government website for the most up-to-date visa requirements and processes, or consult with the nearest UK embassy or consulate in your country.

Visa regulations can change, so it's critical to stay up to date on the newest information.

Allow enough time for visa processing before your scheduled departure date.

Check that your passport is valid for at least six months beyond your expected stay in the UK.

Keep in mind that visa requirements are subject to change owing to a variety of circumstances such as political changes, security concerns, and international agreements.

My Little Experience About my Visa Requirements information

In the midst of everyday life, an extraordinary adventure awaited me in the wonderful city of Liverpool. With excitement in my heart, I set out on a journey to discover the hidden gems of this captivating British gem. However, the way to this incredible vacation began with comprehending the complicated Visa Requirements, which added an aspect of excitement to my travel preparations.

After thoroughly researching the visa restrictions, I was overjoyed to discover that as a tourist, I was eligible for a short-term visit with no issues. The Tourist Visa offered me access to Liverpool's diverse culture and historical landmarks for up to six months, allowing for a completely immersive experience.

With my visa in hand, I arrived in Liverpool and was met by the warm smiles of the residents, their accents weaving a lovely tapestry of hospitality. The city's diversity opened before my eyes as I strolled along its cobblestone streets, admiring beautiful architecture and delighting in the legendary scouse delights.

Liverpool's cultural richness was unsurpassed, as evidenced by its magnificent UNESCO-listed waterfront and the awe-inspiring Beatles heritage. Visiting The Beatles Story museum, I dived into the lives of the renowned band members, relishing in their musical revolution that transformed the globe.

My heart soared as I explored the lively art scene, with galleries like the Tate Liverpool embracing contemporary treasures. The city's sporting zeal captured me as well, as I witnessed the excitement at Anfield, the hallowed grounds of Liverpool Football Club.

In order to better grasp Liverpool's history, I visited museums and magnificent buildings such as the Liverpool Cathedral and St. George's Hall. Each step unearthed enthralling stories that left me wanting more.

Liverpool's nightlife was a sight to behold, with crowded bars and live music venues echoing tunes that imbued the air with a sense of ecstasy. The dynamic environment and camaraderie among the inhabitants made me feel at home, even as a wandering traveler.

Liverpool's allure varies with the seasons. The seaside city provided refreshing retreats to its gorgeous parks and gardens, such as Sefton Park, where I could relax in nature's embrace.

My stay in Liverpool was an immersing journey of self-discovery, with my days spent exploring and my nights filled with partying. The city's rich tapestry of history, art, music, and sports had knitted itself into the fabric of my being.

As my visa expired, I bid a tearful farewell to the enthralling city that had stolen my heart. Liverpool's enchantment persisted in my soul, tempting me to return one day.

Reflecting on my personal experience, I realized that understanding and completing Liverpool's Visa Requirements had made discovering its secrets even more enticing. The tour had given me new friends, memorable memories, and a deep appreciation for this amazing city. Liverpool had touched my soul and sparked an interest in exploring that would accompany me on all future adventures.

Chapter 4 : The Best Cuisine to Try in Liverpool

Prepare to indulge your taste senses in a symphony of sensations that define the city's vibrant culinary environment as you begin on a delicious gourmet adventure across Liverpool. Liverpool's eclectic food culture reflects its rich history and cosmopolitan nature, making it a haven for food-loving travelers looking for a personal and distinctive experience.

Begin your day with a full "Full English Breakfast" at a nearby café, savoring the delectable combination of bacon, sausages, eggs, beans, tomatoes, and black pudding. Head to the renowned Albert Dock for lunch and immerse yourself in the city's maritime past while enjoying a classic bowl of "Scouse," a healthy stew packed with delicious beef, veggies, and a comforting broth.

Allow yourself to be enchanted by the entrancing fragrances of Liverpool's famous "Curry Mile" in the city center as the sun sets. Taste amazing curries, kebabs, and spicy pleasures from India, Pakistan, and Bangladesh.

No trip to Liverpool is complete without sampling the city's famed "Scotch Egg," a wonderful combination of seasoned sausage meat wrapping a soft-boiled egg, fried to perfection and sometimes accompanied with tangy chutneys.

Dive into Liverpool's burgeoning street food scene for a one-of-a-kind and fascinating experience. Wander through lively markets and sample a variety of exotic delicacies, from scrumptious Venezuelan arepas to tantalizing Korean kimchi pancakes.

Head to one of Liverpool's fine dining restaurants for a touch of refinement, where imaginative chefs merge classic British ingredients with modern techniques. Enjoy the creativity on your plate as you savor meals like pan-seared scallops with black pudding, complemented by a refreshing glass of locally made craft beer.

Dessert lovers will find nirvana at the city's bustling patisseries and bakeries, where they may indulge in Liverpool's sweetest gem: the "Liverpool Tart." This exquisite pastry has a shortcrust shell filled with a luscious mixture of currants, butter, sugar, and lemon zest, evoking a perfect symphony of tastes with each bite.

In the midst of your culinary expedition, don't forget to try a classic "Scouse Ale" or "Liver Bird Gin," both locally manufactured beverages that pay homage to Liverpool's history and culture.

As the night progresses, make your way to the legendary "Chinatown" and immerse yourself in a genuine Asian food experience. Delight in meals from China, Malaysia, and beyond, as the brilliant colors and aromatic spices transport you to the bustling streets of the Far East.

Liverpool's vibrant food scene includes vegan and vegetarian options, with a variety of inventive establishments exhibiting plant-based delicacies that appeal to a wide range of palates.
Whether you're a seasoned eater or a curious traveler, Liverpool delivers an unforgettable culinary trip that blends history, culture, and exquisite cuisine. So, let your taste buds go wild, your senses be charmed, and your heart be captivated by the best cuisine that this bustling city has to offer.

Chapter 5: Accommodations in Liverpool and their Cost

As a popular tourist destination, the city provides a diverse choice of lodgings to suit a variety of tastes and budgets. Liverpool has something for everyone, whether you're looking for luxurious hotels, quaint guesthouses, or budget-friendly hostels.

Liverpool has several top-notch hotels in prominent locations for guests wanting a taste of elegance and luxury. Some of the most premium hotels on the city's waterfront provide breathtaking views of the River Mersey and the distinctive Liverpool skyline. These upmarket hotels charge between £150 and £300 per night, depending on the room style and facilities given. Many of these hotels have spas, exercise centers, and outstanding dining selections, making for an enjoyable visit.

There are various mid-range hotels and attractive guest houses sprinkled throughout the city for people on a tight budget. These hotels provide comfortable rooms with modern amenities and are typically priced between £80 and £150 per night. Many of these places are within walking distance of the city's major attractions, making them ideal for travelers wishing to explore the city.

Liverpool's hostels are a good choice for budget-conscious vacationers or backpackers. These hostels have dormitory-style accommodations, individual rooms, and community areas where guests can connect and share travel advice. Hostels are normally priced between £20 to £60 per night, making them an affordable option for young travelers and groups.

Liverpool has also embraced the concept of boutique hotels, which blend flair, comfort, and one-of-a-kind design aspects. These boutique hotels frequently mirror the city's creative and musical legacy, giving guests with an authentic experience. Boutique hotel prices vary depending on location and amenities, but they typically range from £100 to £200 per night.

Liverpool's hotel options are evolving as well. Tourists can now have a more domestic experience while visiting the city, thanks to the rise of vacation rentals and serviced apartments. These self-catering choices are available in a variety of sizes and are ideal for families or tourists looking for a more independent stay.

It is important to note that hotel pricing may vary during busy tourist seasons and major events. It is best to book well in advance to secure the greatest rates and availability. Finding the perfect location to stay in Liverpool is as fascinating as visiting the city's many attractions, with such a broad assortment of hotels to choose from. So, whether you're a history buff, a music fan, or simply looking for an authentic British experience, Liverpool's accommodations are ready to welcome you.

Turkey's location on a map

On the map, Liverpool is a prominent city located in the northwest of England. It is located around 34 miles (55 kilometers) east of the Irish Sea coastline, along the eastern banks of the River Mersey. Liverpool, being a large port city, has historically been a hub for trade, commerce, and cultural exchanges, strengthening its regional relevance.

Liverpool is located in the ceremonial county of Merseyside and covers an area of approximately 43.21 square miles (111.84 square kilometers). Its precise coordinates are 53.4084° N latitude and 2.9916° W longitude. This strategic location has been critical to the city's growth as a bustling marine center, facilitating links with other cities and areas both domestically and globally.

Liverpool, surrounded by a diverse terrain, offers a unique combination of urban charm and natural beauty. The cityscape melts into a patchwork of suburbs to the east, while the western region features a combination of open green spaces, parks, and recreational sites.

Liverpool is today known for its rich history, cultural legacy, and iconic landmarks including the Liver Building, Albert Dock, and Royal Liver Building. As a UNESCO World Heritage Site, the Pier Head's marine mercantile heritage has been safeguarded for future generations. The conserved port system, which showcases the ancient docks and warehouses that have since been transformed as stores, museums, and restaurants, also reflects the city's maritime background.

Furthermore, Liverpool's geographical location has aided its thriving marine and industrial heritage. The city's port has played an important role in establishing its identity, and the Mersey River remains a popular destination for water-based activities such as river cruises and water sports.

Furthermore, Liverpool's geographical location has influenced its climate, which is characterized by warm winters and pleasant summers, as is characteristic of coastal cities. The city has a temperate marine climate with modest rainfall year round.

Chapter 6: Exploring Liverpool's Attractions

We were filled with excitement and anticipation as we began our journey to visit Liverpool's attractions. Our first trip was the famed Liverpool Waterfront, a UNESCO World Heritage Site, where the breathtaking blend of old and modern architecture left us speechless. The Royal Liver Building, the Cunard Building, and the Port of Liverpool Building loomed tall, telling the story of the city's nautical legacy.

Then we went to The Beatles Story, an immersive exhibition that delves into the renowned band's history. We felt like we were a part of their musical journey, from their early days at The Cavern Club to their global renown. We couldn't help but take a photo in front of the famed "Imagine" mosaic in

Strawberry Field, which pays tribute to John Lennon.

The colorful ambiance of Albert Dock drew us in with its art galleries, shops, and eateries. We are excellent local dishes like Scouse and browsed fascinating businesses selling handmade items.

The majesty of Liverpool Cathedral left us awestruck; its architecture and amazing panoramic views from the tower were just breathtaking. While strolling through the revitalized Baltic Triangle, we came across street art, fashionable cafes, and independent businesses.

Of course, a vacation to Liverpool would be nothing without witnessing the city's sporting fanaticism. We cheered on at Anfield, the renowned home of Liverpool FC, soaking in the explosive atmosphere of a football match.

As the sun dropped, we started on a magnificent Mersey River Cruise, watching Liverpool's skyline glisten with lights. The Liver Birds atop the Royal Liver Building seemed to grin towards us, as if saying goodbye to newfound friends.

Liverpool's attractions provided us with an unforgettable experience, combining its rich past, musical legacy, and kind welcome. We left with fond recollections and a commitment to return to this dynamic city that had captured our hearts.

Chapter 7: Museums and Art Galleries in Liverpool

As a tourist exploring Liverpool, I was struck by the city's strong cultural environment, particularly its museums and art galleries. Liverpool has a rich history and a plethora of world-class museums that cater to all interests.

The historic Liverpool Museum, now known as the Museum of Liverpool, took me on a captivating tour through the city's past, showing items and stories spanning generations. From its nautical background to the Beatles' influence, each exhibit was carefully designed to provide an immersive perspective of Liverpool's growth.

As an art aficionado, the Walker Art Gallery was a wonderful paradise for me. The huge collection of paintings and sculptures by renowned painters such as Rembrandt, Turner, and Hockney filled me with amazement and inspiration. The calm atmosphere of the gallery allowed me to fully enjoy each piece.

Another treasure that I treasured was the Tate Liverpool. It was located along the Albert Dock and showcased modern and contemporary art, sparking my imagination with its unique shows and thought-provoking installations.

When I entered the World Museum, I was transported to numerous civilizations and ages. The Egyptian mummies, dinosaur fossils, and interactive scientific exhibits were both educational and amusing, making it a great destination for families.

Exploring the International Slavery Museum, which confronts the atrocities of the transatlantic slave trade, was a highlight of my visit. It was a profound and vital historical lesson that left me reflecting on the importance of human rights and equality.

To round up my museum excursions, I couldn't pass seeing the Beatles Story, an immersive trip into the lives and times of the renowned band. Walking in the footsteps of John, Paul, George, and Ringo, I was enthralled by their music and the impact they had on popular culture.

Liverpool's museums and art galleries were a tribute to the city's commitment to preserve its legacy while welcoming current inventiveness. The varied assortment of attractions catered to every interest and age group. Whether you enjoy history, art, or music, Liverpool's cultural attractions are sure to enlighten and inspire you. I departed with a great appreciation for the city's artistic treasures and the narrative they convey.

8. Liverpool Music and Entertainment

Liverpool, a dynamic city in northwest England, is known for its rich musical legacy and strong entertainment scene. Liverpool, as a popular tourist destination, has a wide range of musical experiences and entertainment opportunities to suit a wide range of preferences and interests.

The Beatles, one of the most recognizable bands in history, are from Liverpool, making the city a must-see for music fans. Tourists can visit The Beatles Story, an immersive museum that chronicles the band's rise from humble beginnings to global superstardom. A visit to the Cavern Club is also required for any Beatles fan. This renowned venue held the band's early performances and continues to host live music acts, ensuring a lively and nostalgic environment.

Aside from The Beatles, Liverpool has a thriving music scene, with various live music venues and clubs distributed around the city. From intimate jazz clubs like "The Jacaranda" to larger concert halls like "Liverpool Philharmonic Hall," there are plenty of options for travelers looking for a fantastic night out.

For individuals interested in classical music, the Liverpool Philharmonic Orchestra routinely conducts classical concerts featuring a wide spectrum of classical masterpieces.

In addition to music, Liverpool provides a varied choice of entertainment for tourists. The city is home to various theaters, notably the huge "Liverpool Empire Theatre," which hosts a range of theatrical acts, musicals, and ballets.

The "Tate Liverpool" has an amazing collection of modern and contemporary art for art enthusiasts.

Another notable attraction is the "Walker Art Gallery," which houses a large collection of European paintings and sculptures.

Families visiting Liverpool can enjoy the "Merseyside Maritime Museum" and the "World Museum," both of which provide intriguing displays for people of all ages.

The "Baltic Triangle" is a lively hub with fashionable pubs, restaurants, and clubs for anyone looking for a taste of the city's nightlife. This vibrant creative quarter frequently holds lively events and festivals that promote local talent.

A journey to Anfield Stadium, the home of Liverpool FC, is a wonderful experience for sports enthusiasts. Tourists can learn about the football club's history by taking a stadium tour and visiting the interactive museum "The Liverpool FC Story."

Finally, visitors may enjoy the bustling ambiance of the "Albert Dock," a historic waterfront complex that houses a variety of restaurants, bars, and stores. The waterfront provides excellent views of the River Mersey and is a favorite area for leisurely walks.

Chapter 9: Outdoor Activities in Liverpool

Liverpool, a city brimming with history, culture, and lively energy, provides a plethora of interesting outdoor activities that will delight any adventurous traveler. As a traveler, I was immediately fascinated by the city's numerous offerings, making it an amazing experience.

Exploring the famous Liverpool Waterfront is one of the attractions. While strolling along the Mersey, I marveled at the spectacular waterfront architecture, which included the famed Liver Building and the Royal Albert Dock. The atmosphere is vibrant, with street performers, bustling marketplaces, and stunning river views.

Sefton Park is a must-see for nature lovers. This large green retreat features tranquil lakes, beautiful gardens, and plenty of space for picnics or leisurely walks. I found peace among the flowering flowers and the magnificent Palm House, a glass conservatory packed with exotic plants.

The city also has amazing water activities. I took a River Explorer Cruise and saw the city from a different angle while learning about Liverpool's nautical history.

I took a Magical Mystery Tour through the Beatles' legacy to get a taste of history and culture. Visiting sites such as Penny Lane and the band members' childhood homes brought their music to life in a unique way.

I went to Anfield Stadium to enjoy Liverpool's sporting spirit. Even if you aren't a sports lover, the electric atmosphere and passionate supporters made it an incredible experience.

Finally, I couldn't resist boarding a ferry to the Wirral Peninsula. The beautiful ride provided breathtaking views of the city and its surrounding environs, making it an ideal opportunity to unwind.

What to Pack

To ensure you're fully prepared to immerse yourself in the magic of this dynamic city, here's a compelling list of what to pack for your Liverpool adventure:

Rain Gear: Embrace Liverpool's weather in style! Pack a stylish umbrella, a waterproof jacket, and comfy waterproof shoes to walk confidently across the city rain or shine.

Fashionable Attire: Liverpool is a city of style, so bring your most fashionable attire for nights out in the hip bars and sparkling clubs.

Beatles Memorabilia: Pay tribute to the Fab Four by bringing over some Beatles stuff. A Beatles t-shirt or memorabilia is a terrific discussion starter with both tourists and locals.

Musical Instruments: Do you have a musical inclination? Bring your guitar or other musical instruments and join the city's busking culture. Strum your way through legendary Beatles tunes along the Albert Dock and street corners, delighting onlookers and relishing in the ambience.

Football Fan Gear: Liverpool is home to two passionate football clubs, so dress in the colors of your favorite team to feel the explosive passion of the locals during match days.

Camera and binoculars: Capture the city's captivating attractions, from the magnificent shoreline to the stunning architecture. Binoculars are ideal for observing prominent sights like the Liver Building in fine detail.

Souvenirs of the Liver Bird: Bring home a piece of Liverpool's identity by purchasing souvenirs of the city's emblem, the Liver Bird, from numerous gift shops.

An Inquisitive Mind: Liverpool is a cultural treasure trove. Pack an adventurous spirit to discover the city's artistic past through its museums, art galleries, and theater.

Travel Journal: Keep track of your travels as you delve into Liverpool's rich history and discover its hidden gems. Fill a travel notebook with your thoughts, capturing the essence of your trip.

Scouse Ingredients: Try the traditional local cuisine, Scouse, by bringing along the ingredients for an original homemade rendition. Engage with the locals, learn their secret recipes, and have a hearty supper.

While cellphones have changed navigation, there's something delightful about unfolding a paper map and a guidebook. They also make lovely souvenirs to remember your vacation.

Sunscreen and sunglasses: When the sun shines in Liverpool, soak up the rays beside the River Mersey or in the city's magnificent parks, so be prepared with sunscreen and stylish shades.

Learn a few Liverpudlian slang phrases to immerse yourself in the city's unique culture. You'll be chatting like a Scouser in no time and making friends with the locals.

Open Mind and friendly Smile: Liverpool is full of friendly, inviting people. Keep an open mind, be ready to engage in discussion, and don't forget to smile!

With this exciting collection of necessities, your Liverpool vacation will be a kaleidoscope of enriching experiences, lovely encounters, and enduring memories. So pack your bags, seize the day, and embark on an exhilarating tour into the heart and soul of Liverpool!

10 Things you can't bring along with you to Liverpool

As a tourist visiting Liverpool, there are numerous fun items you can bring with you to enhance your experience. However, there are a few items you should avoid packing in order to have a pleasant and joyful trip. Here's a fun and useful list of things not to bring:

Umbrellas: Despite the unpredictability of the weather, Liverpool is well-known for its high winds, which may transform an umbrella into a flying hazard! Instead, wear a waterproof jacket.

Doubt: Put your fears aside and enjoy the Scouse spirit! Liverpool is famed for its friendly locals, so come prepared to engage in friendly banter.

Negative stereotypes: Liverpool has a rich cultural legacy, and its people have helped shape the world.

Leave behind any outmoded stereotypes and explore the city with an open mind.

Overstuffed suitcase: Liverpool has wonderful shopping choices, so leave some room in your luggage for souvenirs and one-of-a-kind items.

Weather stereotypes: Yes, Liverpool has its rainy days, but don't let that dampen your spirits. Accept the rain or shine and enjoy the city's charm.

Liverpool is a city rich in music, art, and culture. You'll feel perfectly at home if you sing along, dance in the streets, or interact with street entertainers.

Heels on cobblestones: Liverpool requires comfortable shoes. Leave the high heels at home and settle for something more practical with its historic streets and busy nightlife.

Close-mindedness: Part of what makes Liverpool so fascinating is its cultural diversity. Be open to sampling new meals, discovering new neighborhoods, and appreciating the city's rich history.

A lack of wit: Liverpudlians are known for their wit and humor. Expect to laugh and have a nice time with the locals.

Your Liverpool experience will be memorable and pleasurable if you are conscious of what not to bring and immerse yourself in the city's unique environment. If you embrace the city's ethos, you'll depart with amazing memories and a renewed appreciation for this incredible place.

Health and Safety

As you visit this dynamic city, you can be confident that the local authorities have taken significant precautions to protect your safety.

Liverpool takes great pride in its health and safety efforts, which make it a safe and enjoyable visitor destination. The city's transportation system is well-kept and easily accessible, with regular inspections and safety precautions in place. Take advantage of the numerous pedestrian-friendly zones and well-marked crosswalks that encourage safe walking exploration.

Liverpool maintains excellent cleaning standards in public spaces, constantly disinfecting public facilities and commonly touched surfaces. Hand sanitizing facilities are carefully located for your convenience and to promote good hygiene practices.

The city's restaurants and cafes rigorously comply with health and safety requirements, guaranteeing that you may enjoy the wonderful cuisine of Liverpool with confidence. Look for the 'Food Hygiene Rating Scheme' labels, which indicate a restaurant's adherence to hygiene requirements.

If you have any medical issues, Liverpool has excellent healthcare services. Your health is well-cared for, from well-equipped hospitals to dependable pharmacies. Don't forget to obtain comprehensive travel insurance before your trip to provide you extra peace of mind while you're away.

It's usually a good idea to be cautious and aware of your surroundings when traveling. Liverpool is a friendly community, but it's important to keep attentive and follow general safety precautions.

Remember that when exploring the attractions of Liverpool, your health and safety are of the utmost importance. So, unwind and enjoy everything this wonderful city has to offer!

Travel Costs

If you're visiting as a tourist, prepare for an extraordinary experience that will leave you with fond memories and a wish to return.

Don't be concerned about trip expenses! Liverpool has a wide variety of products to suit all budgets. Hostels and cheap hotels abound for the frugal tourist, offering pleasant and economical lodgings without sacrificing quality. There are upmarket hotels and boutique accommodations with superb service and spectacular views if you want a touch of luxury.

The well-connected public transportation infrastructure in Liverpool makes exploring the city a breeze. Consider obtaining a Liverpool Day Saver, which allows you unlimited travel on buses, trains, and ferries, allowing you to easily transition from the historic Albert Dock to the famed Beatles Story.

Liverpool's cuisine culture is a delight for foodies. The city caters to all tastes and budgets, offering everything from traditional British fish and chips to exotic delights. Don't miss out on a delicious Scouse stew in one of the small neighborhood taverns.

Exciting landmarks such as the historic Liver Building, the magnificent Metropolitan Cathedral, and the World Museum are frequently free to attend, making it simple to immerse yourself in Liverpool's rich culture without breaking the budget.

When it comes to entertainment, Liverpool's vibrant music and nightlife culture is legendary. Catch a live performance at The Cavern Club, where the Beatles once performed, and dance the night away in the city's hip clubs.

Liverpool's retail possibilities are numerous, ranging from the bustling Liverpool ONE shopping mall to quirky local stores on Bold Street.

Visit the famed Maritime Museum in Liverpool to learn about the city's maritime legacy and its role in the Titanic disaster.

10 Saving Tips

As a fellow tourist who has experienced the wonderful city of Liverpool, I've compiled some useful saving suggestions to make your visit both memorable and cost-effective. Liverpool is well-known for its rich history, prominent landmarks, and vibrant culture. Here are ten money-saving ideas to improve your experience:

City Explorer Pass: Purchase a City Explorer Pass, which provides free or cheap admission to popular attractions such as the Beatles Story, Liverpool Cathedral, and more.

Free Museums and Galleries: Liverpool is home to various free museums and galleries, including the Tate Liverpool and the World Museum, which offer an insight into the city's art and history.

Albert Dock: Take a stroll around the gorgeous Albert Dock for free and soak in the charming ambiance.

Walking Tours: Join free walking tours conducted by locals to discover the city's hidden beauties and learn about its interesting history.

Mersey Ferry: Enjoy spectacular views of the city's waterfront on a low-cost Mersey Ferry journey.

Economical Eateries: Sample delicious yet reasonable local cuisine at bustling food markets like the Baltic Market, or stroll to the side streets for budget-friendly cafes and eateries.

Accommodation: For low-cost lodging, consider staying in cheap hostels or booking private vacation rentals through services like Airbnb.

To navigate the city, take use of low-cost public transit choices such as buses or the Merseyrail.

Pre-purchase Tickets: Save money on admission and avoid long lines by purchasing tickets in advance for popular attractions and events.

Parks & Gardens: Unwind in the city's wonderful parks and gardens, such as Sefton Park and Calderstones Park, which provide tranquil getaways at no cost.

My own experience in Liverpool was simply amazing. The city's welcoming environment and rich musical tradition, notably the Beatles' legacy, left an indelible impression on me. I had a great time exploring the docks, admiring the gorgeous architecture, and learning about the local culture. The Liverpudlian enthusiasm is intoxicating, and I found myself engaging in chats with pleasant residents, obtaining insider recommendations and hidden gems to explore. I enjoyed live music events and comedy clubs as part of the city's bustling nightlife.

To make the most of your trip while saving money, take advantage of the city's free attractions, savor reasonable culinary pleasures, and choose efficient transit alternatives. By following these money-saving ideas, you'll not only make cherished memories but also keep your budget intact, creating a really unforgettable stay in Liverpool.

As a devoted traveler who has explored Liverpool's beautiful options, I can't help but share my fantastic experience with romantic hotels for couples in this bustling city. Liverpool, with its rich history and dynamic culture, is an ideal place for lovebirds looking for a memorable holiday.

The exquisite 30 James Street Hotel - Home of the Titanic is one of Liverpool's most sought-after romantic hotels. This luxurious hotel on the city's famous waterfront offers breathtaking views of the River Mersey and the iconic Three Graces. Its exquisite and spacious suites are decorated in historical style, giving a sense of timeless romance. The on-site rooftop patio is a lovely setting for romantic nights spent watching the sunset with your loved one.

Another hidden gem is The Shankly Hotel, named after Liverpool FC icon Bill Shankly. This hotel combines modern luxury with football heritage, with elegant rooms and an engaging ambiance. Couples can enjoy a relaxing spa treatment or cocktails at the beautiful Garden of Eden rooftop bar, which overlooks the metropolitan skyline.

A night's stay at these romantic hotels can cost between £150 and £300, depending on the room style and season. However, the experience is absolutely priceless. Liverpool's rich culture, exciting nightlife, and historic buildings will leave you and your companion with cherished memories that last a lifetime. Whether you're strolling hand in hand along the Albert Dock or sharing a nice candlelit dinner at one of the city's top-notch restaurants, Liverpool will kindle the sparks of passion, making it a perfect location for couples seeking an unforgettable trip.

Day 1: Welcome to Liverpool!

Arrive in Liverpool and settle into your pleasant lodging. Begin your adventure with a guided walking tour of the city's core. Explore the historic Albert Dock, which is home to renowned institutions such as the Merseyside Maritime Museum and the Beatles Story. Immerse yourself in the city's musical past and learn about the rise of the Fab Four. Finish your day with a wonderful lunch at one of the fashionable eateries along the waterfront.

Day 2: Liverpool's Cultural Treasures

Today, embark on a cultural adventure by visiting the Walker Art Gallery, which has a remarkable collection of European art. Then, proceed to St. George's Hall, a neoclassical masterpiece with a beautiful interior. Take a ferry across the Mersey River to experience stunning views of the city. In the evening, watch a performance by the Royal Liverpool Philharmonic Orchestra for a dose of classical music.

Day 3: Examine the Beatles' Legacy

Today, go deeper into the Beatles' world by visiting The Cavern Club, where the band memorably performed. Continue your journey to Mendips and 20 Forthlin Road, the childhood residences of John Lennon and Paul McCartney. Explore The Beatles Statue at Pier Head and take a great shot. Finish the day with an incredible Beatles-themed evening of live music at one of the many pubs they frequented.

Day 4: Day Trip to Chester

Take a day excursion to the charming city of Chester, which is only a short train ride from Liverpool. Walk along the medieval city walls and marvel at the half-timbered Rows. Visit Chester Cathedral and immerse yourself in the history and beauty of this wonderful city. Return to Liverpool and treat yourself with a taste of the famed Scouse cuisine at a typical pub.

Day 5: Anfield Stadium & Maritime History

Football fans must not pass up the opportunity to visit Anfield Stadium, the iconic home of Liverpool FC. Take a guided tour of the stadium and learn about the club's rich history. The Merseyside Maritime Museum, which includes the Titanic display, is a must-see for maritime aficionados. In the evening, enjoy the pulsating nightlife on Seel Street and the buzzing vitality of the city.

Day 6: Relaxing at Sefton Park

Spend a relaxing day at Sefton Park, one of Liverpool's most lovely green spaces. Stroll around the tranquil boating lake, see the Palm House, and enjoy a delicious picnic. On weekends, explore the surrounding Lark Lane, which is full with eccentric cafes, vintage shops, and handmade boutiques. This is an excellent opportunity to unwind and learn about the local culture.

Day 7: River Cruise and Farewell

Finish your Liverpool experience with a gorgeous Mersey river cruise. Take in the city's skyline from a new angle and take some great photos. Explore intriguing exhibits from all over the world at the World Museum. Before you leave Liverpool, eat a final lunch at one of the city's top restaurants, reminiscing on the fantastic experiences you've had during your visit.

Liverpool delivers an intriguing blend of culture, music, history, and friendly hospitality. If you embrace this interesting city, you will have lasting recollections of your journey.

Getting a Map

Obtaining a map in Liverpool is a vital tool for any tourist looking to make the most of their visit. Fortunately, the city gives various possibilities for obtaining maps.

When you arrive at Liverpool John Lennon Airport or the central train station, you'll discover information centers with free maps and brochures. These useful brochures include full city plans, highlighting landmarks such as The Beatles Story Museum, Liverpool Cathedral, and the historic Albert Dock.

Consider downloading the "Explore Liverpool" app, which is available for iOS and Android. This interactive map not only provides directions but also audio guides and historical information about significant spots. Another option is to go to the Liverpool Tourist Information Center, which is located in the center of the city and offers high-quality maps as well as individual advice from knowledgeable staff.

With your map in hand, explore the compelling blend of modern and old architecture, wander along the gorgeous waterfront, and immerse yourself in the vibrant music scene that gave rise to the Beatles. Don't forget to visit the diverse neighborhoods, each with its own distinct charm and cultural offers.

Allow the map to be your trusted companion as you explore this fascinating city, guiding you on a memorable trip through Liverpool's past and present. Allow the magic of this maritime city to seduce you!

Conclusion

As we near the end of this Liverpool Travel Guide, we are swamped with memories of this vibrant and engaging city. Throughout these chapters, we've looked at the beating heart of Liverpool, a city that pulsates with history, culture, and a really unique soul.

We discovered a tale ready to be told in every area of Liverpool. Liverpool stands as a tribute to the dreams and aspirations of generations past and present, from the landmark Albert Dock, where echoes of the city's maritime past resound through time, to the grand churches that decorate the skyline.

We wandered through the Georgian Quarter's quaint streets, where each building seemed to whisper secrets of a bygone era, and we danced through the bustling energy of Bold Street, where the aroma of diverse cuisines from around the world enticed us to indulge in a culinary adventure unlike any other.

But, behind the buildings and architecture, the genuine spirit of Liverpool can be found - its people. The Scousers' excitement for their city knows no bounds, and they are kind, hospitable, and full of life. We were welcomed as honorary Liverpudlians, from the local bar chats to the applause at Anfield, and we felt a sense of belonging that made our journey unique.

We don't only visit places as travelers; we seek out experiences that shape us. Liverpool is one such transforming environment. Its rich cultural past, illustrated by the Beatles' legacy and the thriving artistic scene, penetrates the very soul of anyone fortunate enough to walk its streets.

This book was created with passion, driven by a desire to share the beauties of Liverpool with fellow travelers seeking an immersive voyage of discovery rather than just a vacation. We hope it has inspired you to walk along the Mersey, to watch the sunset over the Liver Building, and to relish the serendipity that awaits you around every corner.

Remember to retain an open heart and mind when you close this book and embark on your own adventure across Liverpool. Allow yourself to become lost in the charming alleyways and accept the unexpected encounters that will definitely enhance your trip.

Liverpool's allure persists long after you leave, and it will always have a special place in your heart. So, my traveler, go forth and immerse yourself in Liverpool's wonders. Accept its history, accept its people, and let this city of miracles make an unforgettable imprint on your soul.

May your journey be full of joy, amazement, and memories that you will cherish for the rest of your life. Thank you for entrusting us with your vacation experience, and may you always return to Liverpool's soul-stirring embrace.

Safe Travels and Exciting adventures!

Printed in Great Britain
by Amazon